# MAXIMIZING MENTALLY

Written By:
Raymond Forte

© 2020 by
Raymond Forte

All rights reserved. No part of this book may be reproduced in any form without permission in writing from the publisher, except in the case of brief quotations embodied in critical articles or reviews. No part of this publication may be reproduced, stored in a retrieval system, or transmitted in any form or by any means, electronic, mechanical, recording or otherwise, without the prior written permission of the author.

Scripture quotations are taken from the *Holy Bible*, New Living Translation, copyright ©1996, 2004, 2007 by Tyndale House Foundation; the *Holy Bible,* King James Version. New York: American Bible Society: 1999 Holy Bible, King James Version, copyright © 1999 by New York: Bible Society; and the *Holy Bible,* Amplified Version, *Copyright © 2015.*

Printed in the United States of America

THIS BOOK IS NOT INTENDED TO BE A HISTORY TEXT. While every effort has been made to check the accuracy of dates, locations, and historical information, no claims are made as to the accuracy of such information.

INFORMATION IN THIS BOOK DOES NOT REPRESENT THE VIEWS OF DUDLEY PUBLISHING HOUSE OR ANY OF IT'S SUBSIDAIRIES.
For book orders, author appearance inquires and interviews, contact author:

ISBN-978-0-9988025-8-9

Dudley Publishing House

# Dedication

Dedicated to my mother, brothers, CH3, and the people that believed in me.

# Content

Chapter 1 - "Maximizing MENtally" in our *Identity*

Chapter 2 - "Maximizing MENtally" from *Injury*

Chapter 3- "Maximizing MENtally" in *Isolation*

Chapter 4 - "Maximizing MENtally" in our *Independence*

Chapter 5 - "Maximizing MENtally" and our *Impact*

# Forward

"And I will put enmity Between you and the woman, And between your seed and her Seed; He shall bruise your head, And you shall bruise His heel." (Genesis 3:15 KJV).

It is universally agreed that the sin of Adam resulted in enmity being placed between Satan and the woman's seed. Scripture plainly says "and between your seed and her seed." While there is agreement that enmity was placed, there are different views regarding the seed. Is the seed the woman? Is the seed a prophecy of the virgin birth? Is the seed a reference to the woman's descendants, particularly her male descendants? Because we see through a glass darkly, this is one of those questions that we will ultimately settle in eternity. In the meantime, let's conclude that the seed refers to the male descendants of the first woman, Eve. The male has faced fierce

enmity with Satan since the Genesis of time. The male is the seed and he uniquely carry seed which puts us in direct opposition to Satan. He's after the seed.

One of the areas that Satan uses to attack the male is in his mind. Whenever a man gains victory in his mind he will have victory over his life. A man's life is maximized when he maximizes it mentally. In Maximizing Mentally, Raymond Forte demonstrates a level of honesty and transparency rarely expressed by men. He testifies of his own struggles of the past and how he was able to overcome. His sports fanaticism and illustrations offer an added appeal to the male audience. Few, if any, will read Maximizing Mentally and not be able to relate in some way. This book has the potential to save many lives. His story is not isolated. He has allowed us to peer into his own mental challenges in hopes that those who read it will get the help they need.

Enjoy life to the max as you maximize mentally.

Bishop Jerry Hutchins

# Introduction

Many men are desperately crying for resources to help them in the area of mental health. If we look at recent stories in society, we have seen and continue to see more and more cases of men who have committed crimes that were a direct result of mental health from murdering the people closest to them; to taking matters into their own hands and committing suicide.

In recent history, there have been many cases of men committing crimes of homicide and even suicide as a direct result of mental health issues. On February 11,

2019, I experienced the worst mental breakdown ever. I moved on to Phoenix, AZ better known as the "Valley of the Sun" to work for a well-known organization only to later lose the position

Feeling alone and abandoned, I felt a sense of desolation that had me at my lowest point. However, on that day that I decided that I would not be silent any longer about my mental health. I committed to, not only help myself, but others who are incarcerated in their prison of mental health issues.

In this book, *Maximizing MENtally*, I want to let every man reading this know that he is not alone. I dare not say that this is the end-all-be-all book that will answer every question. However, understanding that this book will outlast me, I know there will be more men that will need a resource that allows them to feel like someone hears their voice. I intend for this to be that resource. Purchasing this book, *Maximizing MENtally* is a sign that healing is a priority. However, I would urge you to locate a local therapist so that you can process what you've experienced properly.

  I'm not sure if anyone has told you this but I'm proud of you for taking a step towards healing. It's never easy to say that you need help, especially as a man. We pride ourselves in making sure we can keep everything together; however, there are times when you are going to need someone to understand the struggles that you face as a man. It is my prayer that this book speaks to you in a way where you are encouraged to keep going and to face the issues that you are challenged with so you can come out strong and on top. Welcome to your journey of *Maximizing MENtally*.

# *Identity*

Let me preface our conversation by informing you that I am a huge sports fan — a die-hard at that. So you'll be seeing in this book a lot of comparisons to the sports and players I love. The purpose of my illustrations are to apply the points I need to make for the goal of the book to be met, ensuring that we are *Maximizing MENtally* in every area of our life. With that being said, let's begin this journey.

## Maximizing MENtally | Raymond Forte

Every man is shaped by his identity. Little boys desperately seek his uniqueness from the man he considers most significant in his life. The name little boys are given shape their identity and what they are destined to be. He is shaped by who influences him the most.

Last year, I did an intense study on the late Kobe Bryant and his unmatched work ethic. His enthusiasm for the game of basketball was and still is an inspiration to watch even in his death. I went back to old videos of his style of play and how he approached the game and it is like watching Michael Jordan in a different form. He wanted to be identified with the best and learn from the best so he emulated Jordan's style and took on his mentality to win, this is why Kobe is acknowledged as one of the 50 greatest players to ever play in the National Basketball Association.

When a man understands his identity, he is laser-focused on what it is that he has used to classify himself. The greatest key you can take away from any man at any age is his individuality.

My name, Raymond, is German for protector. My middle name, Justin, is the Anglicized Latin version of the word justice. I am shaped by how I'm named and it took me years to find this out. Since I can remember, I've always had a protective nature. When I was married to my former wife, I raised three girls with her which meant I had to be more protective. In addition to that, I'm a fighter for those who are not being treated fairly when it comes to justice. When a man discovers his identity, it greatly disturbs the pits of hell and those who can't recognize their own God-given personality.

Let's look at David. He was a very skillful musician and was great at what he did. His skill level and humility had an entire city singing his praises, this disturbed his boss,

Saul. Although Saul had a position over David, he lost the power, or anointing, that he once had when he first sat in the position as king (1 Samuel 19 NIV). When a man knows his identity, he will find a way to use his gift to make room for him against all the odds. We must allow the next generation of boys that we are rearing to find their identity as they are becoming men.

Unfortunately, we live in a society that tries to box the identity of a man based on his educational and economic status. While this is important for men to realize, there is a pool of men, including myself, that had or have secret struggles with who he is and how God has created him. As a boy, I grew up with both parents in the home until I was 13, and when my parents split, I made the unfortunate decision to live with my father because of anger towards my mother. Although my father was present, he lacked identity which created years of trauma and severe dysfunction in the Forte household. A mentally sick and broken man because of how he was reared and his own traumatic upbringing, he was secretly and at times desperately-determined for his sons not to know who they were or pursue what they wanted because he didn't know who he was. Abusive and abrasive, my dad did whatever he could to keep us under his control and to do what he wanted us to do instead of allowing us to have a choice of what we wanted to do. He would use fear tactics, verbal, mental and physical abuse to get us to follow his unfortunately demonic and dangerous leadership as the man of the house. I'll give you an example. I've always been a lover of music, media and sports. He wanted my brothers and I to live out his music dream that he never accomplished so that he could live through us, which was extremely uncomfortable for me. Whenever I expressed my interest in doing something outside of his dream, his anger would get so out of control that I suppressed a lot of my feelings of anger and stagnation. I could not speak up about what I wanted to do outside of what he envisioned for my brothers and I. Talk about a deep level of control.

Whenever I spoke up about what I liked to do outside of his view of us, he would embarrass and insult me as if I offended him. I hated him for it and still struggle with whether or not I fully forgive him. As a result, I've spent many years struggling with who I was because my identity was in the hands of a broken man who didn't know his own identity. He used his lack of knowing himself to punish me by calling me all types of names that I wouldn't dare type out in words. But let's say it's something that you would not want to call another.

Because my personality was extroverted and I wasn't the most masculine teenager, he would frequently accuse me of being gay calling me derogatory names and making dysfunctional assumptions that I was soft or weak. To disprove these accusations, I lost my virginity two weeks before I turned 16 to a woman nine years my elder. I did it to try to break the view of my father, brothers and those around me that I was not gay, plus my mother was not present because I was living with my dad, who at the time was not the protector or provider he needed to be. He was too sick mentally and physically to raise teenage boys; instead he tried to control them. Losing my virginity was a way of escape from the external circumstances surrounding me. It was not right, and it contributed to so many of my failed relationships with women. No fault of anyone else, I had to be healed from that and acknowledge that it played a major factor in my view of sexuality and why I abused it.

For years I struggled with my own identity trying to prove something to people that did not have the final determination of my destiny or the depth thereof. Struggling with my identity in God as an adult, I wanted to do everything I could to please the people closest to me. I went at length to appease those who felt I should be what they envisioned for my life and abused it by becoming very promiscuous trying to prove to everyone else, and secretly my late father, that I was not the gay man that they thought I was. This is not a jab at the LGBTQ community as I have friends who love the same gender. However, my need to prove that I was not a homosexual man destroyed my identity even further. Rather than being what God called me to be and finding myself secure and comfortable in that, I began to exhibit behaviors that were in direct opposition. This caused my ministry and reach to be less effective and limited. These behaviors also destroyed my marriage as my continuous cheating and promiscuity were too much for my former wife to handle. My lack of identity brought a level of disarray and chaos. I had no focus and was destroying the resources and relationships that were afforded to me.

This resulted in experiencing my biggest fear, becoming like my deceased father. It took me almost losing everything, even my mind, to realize that my identity was not predicated on what everyone else wanted me to be, but my identity is who God formed me to be. So many times, men are pressured into being what everyone wants them to be instead of digging deep to discover who and how God made them at their core. I'm sure countless men are reading this who feel trapped in a false identity. One that has made them believe that there is no way out of that dysfunctional way of thinking. But my friend and brother, you can rediscover who you are in Christ without tagging a salary or position to yourself. David, without playing a single instrument, was anointed when Samuel visited the house even though his father, Jesse, denied and never named him when asked about another son. You may not have had your father give you your identity but when you seek the Father, He will give you an identity that no person can ever take from you. As we move on to the next chapter, allow me to say in closing that your IDENTITY is connected to your AUTHORITY as a man. Walk in it.

# 2

## *Injury*

The worst thing that could happen to any athlete is a career-threatening injury. It's heartbreaking to see, especially when it is serious. It affects the organization, fan base, and often, the city that the player plays in. Some physical injuries are quicker to recover from but there are some mental and emotional injuries that are harder to overcome.

In my life, I've experienced two major physical injuries. When I was 11, I broke my right hand while playing flag football in school, and when I was 13, I broke my foot while wrestling with one of my younger brothers that left me on crutches for a month. Both affected me greatly, yet I recovered from those much quicker and easier than I did the emotional injuries that took years for healing and recovery. The psychological drama that was an everyday occurrence in our household living with my father was a mental nightmare for me. Every day, it seemed as if he woke up angry with the world, his wife (my mother) and his boys. It seemed as if he was satisfied with injuring us with his words and actions but not only that, allowing others to injure us.

The first form of physical, emotional and mental injury first happened when I was a lad playing drums. It was my father who inflicted the pain. The church youth choir I was playing for went on a trip to sing at an outside event, about an hour from where we lived. When we arrived, I realized that I left my drum sticks at the church. My father became so angry that he embarrassed and humiliated me by yelling, screaming, grabbing me by the arms and shaking me to the point that some of the other church members had to step in and stop him. He was so aggressive and could have seriously injured me. This experience haunted me for years and shaped me to fear him in a way that was unhealthy and dysfunctional. There was a time in the summer of 2002 when we were living with our father that affected me for years. One of my brothers answered a phone call from our mother, whom we were forbidden to speak to because he was so angry that she divorced him, he used us as pawns to hurt her. When he found this out, he took every piece of glass that he could find and broke it all destroying our apartment because of my brother's conversation with my mom.

This injured me psychologically for a long time. I had never seen anyone get so angry to the point of destroying an entire apartment. Later that day, my father told his girlfriend what happened and she sided with him. After she found out, she picked me and my brothers up and took us to her son's house 10 minutes away, who was a police officer for the Dekalb County. He punished us by forcing us to do military-style exercises because of my father's dysfunctional thinking and ways of raising sons. As a teenager, I felt helpless and vulnerable. I felt less than human being as this adult was using his authority to punish children that he did not know, and who did nothing that deserved that type of punishment. To add insult to injury, all of this was done to me and my brothers while we were doing ministry and singing as a gospel group. I was angry at God, my mother, my father and the adults that I felt should have protected my brothers and I because we were boys that were living their life. It affected every part of my life, even until adulthood. That event, along with others, took me years to recover from, and I had to fully forgive every adult that did not protect me without an apology.

There are some emotional and psychological injuries that many men, no matter how rich or famous they are, haven't recovered from. Some had the emotional injury of an absentee father or the mental injury of a verbally abusive mother. As men, we must be careful with our children as it relates to their emotional health. We must watch the words we say, the actions we exhibit, and the company we keep. As fathers know, we can't protect our children from every injury; however, it is our duty to cover and protect them from any injury that is potentially caused by us. My heart breaks for the men who are too broken and embarrassed to say what or who hurt them. We often are told not to express when we are hurt. When we take a hit, we are told to suck up our tears and get back up. While I do advocate forward movement in life, some injuries take time to heal. Men, I urge you if you are hurting emotionally, find someone safe to talk to about it. Many of us hurt others because we've been hurt.

This is a troublesome confession for me, both of my parents sadly hurt me. My mother hurt me because I felt she should have intervened in our defense when my father recklessly and continuously put us in harm's way on every end. I was even more hurt by and lost a lot of respect for my father as a man because he did not have our best interests at heart as he should've been, in my eyes, the protector and provider we needed him to be as his sons. Even in that, I could not heal from the injury of my anger without getting the necessary care and properly heal. And by proper care, I mean *therapy*.

Some men are reading this who feel they don't have the time or resources to get help. This is understandable speaking from experience. For years when I was married and working 3 or 4 jobs trying to provide, I felt like I could not recover from what mentally hurt me. So I worked more to mask the pain only for it to result in crazy decision making. I heard a quote from a widely popular preacher that said these mind-shattering words, "Hurt is neither right nor wrong; it's REAL." When men hurt, we often try to cover it because we are told to cover it up. However, some injuries take time to heal.

Here's an example why healing from injuries is imperative for the man that's reading this and who wants to *Maximize MENtally* in this season of their life. During the 2019 NBA playoffs, Kevin Durant experienced a career threatening calf injury in game 5 of the Western Conference semifinals against the Houston Rockets. When the doctor saw the nature of the injury, he said it was more serious than he thought and recommended that Durant be out for a certain period of time in order to recover. This meant he would need to miss the remainder of the playoffs. However, he experienced a greater injury earlier in the season that sent shockwaves around the NBA and the general public. He was disrespected by his teammate, Draymond Green, star forward at the time of the Golden State Warriors. Green accused Durant of not being fully committed to the team because he was in the final year of his contract and was not vocal about his next move as a free agent once the season was completed. That incident alongside having to deal with the pressure from his teammates and media to try to prove his loyalty to his team, he decided to play even though his calf was not fully healed. Coming back for game 5 of the NBA Finals in a joyous mood firing up his teammates and the city that so desperately wanted him to win, he seemed as if he was fully ready to compete unhealed. He was able to make a huge difference in the first half, lifting his team to the second quarter. But as he was driving to the lane, defended by Serge Ibanka, he re-injured his calf, causing him to miss the entire 2019-2020 NBA season with his new team, the Brooklyn Nets.

Many men, young and old, are working injured, preaching injured, praying while injured, and succumbing to pressure from outside influences to get back into full swing. However, we can not allow the pressure of people who don't feel our pain not to prevent us from fully recovering.

    Yes, we will lose occasionally. Yes, we will miss out on some things. But recovery from emotional injuries of our past is crucial. They affect everything and everyone around us. More importantly, we have to get healed for ourselves. If we don't, the healing doesn't begin which will create a barrier for your breakthrough.

It's okay to say you've been hurt from an injury, but it's not okay to stay hurt. Get up and heal; it's better in the end. It will cost you something but more importantly, you will gain your freedom and mind back. It's time to *Maximize MENtally* and recover from any injury that stifled you.

.

# 3

## *Trust the Process*

Isolation is defined as a cause or reason to be set apart from others. For men, this can be a scary thing. The worst thing for a man to feel is alone. As a matter of fact, the Bible teaches us in Genesis 2:18a that, "It is not good for man to be alone." Here's a secret that a lot of men don't admit: we don't want to be alone. Being apart from others can cause men to act out in ways that lead to life-altering consequences including incarceration.

However, I would argue that sometimes, in order to *Maximize MENtally* there are some seasons when we need to be in a place of isolation. God does His best work with us when we are alone and in direct communion with Him. There are times in our lives when God has to remove the things, people and connections we once had so that we can hear His voice and instruction.

When Moses was leading the people to the promised land, he needed time to be alone to pray to God for instruction. In the book of Psalms, David referred to being in the valley of the shadow of death. He also alluded to being forsaken by his mother and father and asked God in the Psalms, why was he forsaken. Jesus even had a place of isolation right after He was baptized by John the Baptist. He spent 40 days in the wilderness before He performed His first miracle. Whenever Jesus would need to get refreshed after performing a miracle or doing ministry, He would go to a place alone so that he could pray and center himself for ministry. Proper isolation in many ways is necessary for the man to create his best work.

I, myself, needed time to be isolated from certain people. This was one of the most traumatic experiences in my adulthood. People who I thought would be around slowly distanced themselves from me. I don't say that to say I haven't made my share of bad decisions in my relationships, there are choices I made that caused people to walk away. However, it was good for me to experience the isolated experience because of the effect it had on me. It allowed me to reflect on how I got there and what I needed to do to mature me for manhood.

You will not always be isolated but there will come a time and season that requires you to be set apart so that you can refocus and reflect on where your life has gone and where you want your life to go. I'm not where I want to be; however, isolation allowed me to hear God in ways that I hadn't heard Him before. It built my discernment and allowed me to see who was on my side and who was trying to pierce me in my side.

Let me dig a little bit deeper with the word *isolation*. As I've stated, I am a lover of sports and of those sports is basketball. For years, I heard the term *isolation*, but did not understand what it meant in basketball. When I found out, it blew me away.

Isolation plays in basketball are offensive plays designed to create one-on-one game situations, utilizing a team's best player. *ISO* plays are great in the end game when there is little time left on the game clock in the 4th quarter.

Players tend to get creative with their dribble in isolation. They do things to try to throw the defender off balance. In isolation, you have permission to be as creative and instinctive as possible because it's you and the real enemy: *the inner me.*

There were periods in my life where God had me in isolation, but I spent so much time *complaining* that I failed to be *creative*.

I spent so much time being distracted by my isolation rather than embracing the moment that was divinely set up by God so that I could seek him and He would bring the best out of me. I spent so much energy trying to become famous in this world, and now I'm convinced I wanted to be even more popular in hell with the crap I indulged in. Ha! It wasn't until I lost everything that I realized the consequences of my every move while in isolation. One wrong move and the defender can steal possession at any given moment. This could cost you the game; and in some cases the season.

The greatest moments are made when it seems as if we are in isolation. But it is, in essence, a set up for the big stage so that God can present a ready vessel of a man to bring the world right-side up. Isolation does not always feel good but God uses isolation for our good.

As a kid growing up, I felt isolated from every circle because I would see other kids with functional working fathers. They were making great strides in their academics and social settings while we had to carry my father from pillar to post. I felt isolated because I felt as if I was loved by everyone else at times, but my father-based on his love of how well he could live vicariously through me and my brothers. If that was unsuccessful, then he expressed in a very traumatic way that he didn't love us. Yeah, that wasn't love at all. As a teenager, I would often hear the fathers closest to me talk about how they want the best for their kids, yet I was being controlled and verbally abused by my own. I felt isolated because I had to go above and beyond to prove my loyalty to him abandoning my dreams and denying my own identity. I felt isolated, but I believe that God was using those moments to build and shape me.

I will say however, I needed to deal with my isolation seasons with a therapist after experiencing such a horrific mental break down on February 11, 2019. My constant fear of isolation brought me to a screeching halt in life. Once I realized why God uses isolation, I was able to better maximize my time during those seasons. In isolation, I wrote this book. It took God isolating me so that I could focus on what was in me; rather than focus on what others outside of me thought. I was able to discover my true value in the seasons of isolation. I needed to discover not just another job; but my gift and my purpose.

One of my favorite players who dominated those isolation plays was Allen Iverson. His creativity in isolation is one that could never be duplicated. The way he would have fun with his feet and be creative with his dribble enamored me every time I watched him play. I've had the pleasure of seeing him twice in person. The way he would entertain the now State Farm Arena with his creativity in isolation is the reason why tickets would nearly be sold out every time he visited Atlanta where I lived at the time. Another reason why I enjoyed watching him was because he was a giant killer. He was able to look his defender in the eye one on one and show fearlessness for his team and the city that he represented. One of my favorite moments by him was the 2001 NBA Finals when his Philadelphia 76ers were against the Los Angeles Lakers who were undefeated in the playoffs that year. The score was 101-99 with under a minute of play and Iverson had possession of the ball to set up an isolation play between him and Tyrone Lue. He was able to look at his defender, on a national stage, being the underdog, size him up, cross him over, score the basket and step over his defender.

For some of the men reading this, God, your head Coach, has created an isolation play for you because he knows you're capable of the situation in crunch time. Isolation is a time that exposes you in a way that separates you from the men and the boys. You find out more about yourself when God causes you to be alone for a season. Our God knows that in isolation, you're going to be able to defeat the giant that seems unbearable. He will never coach you in the wrong direction because He's setting you up to win. Your family, friends and the lives you're going to impact are affected by how you handle the season of isolation.

# 4

## *Free Your Mind*

Every man desire to be independent way before he's even mature enough to handle that level of responsibility. Teenage boys in particular, believe that they can handle the responsibilities of adulthood just because they may have a job and can pay some type of rent or simply because they've turned 16. I'm sure most - if not all - men have uttered these words "I'm a man," at some point before their 18th birthday. Oftentimes, they have no clue of what it takes to run an entire household. When I was a teenager, I thought I knew what it took, but I had no idea until I became an adult. But let's not get away from the point. The reason most men want independence is because of the innate desire to be providers. That's how we are naturally made. When a man is able to provide for himself, and able to take care of all the bills, he's taken more seriously in society.

However, men must not get to a place of arrogance in our pursuit of independence. As much as we are able to take care of ourselves, we must ultimately remember that we are still submitted to the God of the resources. *He* is our Source. We must remember that we can't get so far away from the Father; and become so independent that we stop seeking His direction. Just like the prodigal son; he was able to take care of himself because of the inheritance that was given to him by his father, which was equal to his death. But because of a lack of wisdom and maturity coupled with his independence, the prodigal son was found in a pig pen practicing his apology so that he could be accepted by his father again.

I mentioned my love for Allen Iverson's toughness and creativity. But what I admire about him more than even in his greatness, talent, skill level or influence is that he had enough sense and humility to submit to a coach. In an interview with Stephen A. Smith, Iverson talks about his respect for Larry Brown who was his head coach during his tenure with the Philadelphia 76ers. In the interview, Iverson was asked how he felt about Brown and he answered, "He taught me, he got me ready. He helped me learn that you ain't always right." When a man of greatness is able to submit himself, in his independence, to instruction of the right voice, he is able to go far beyond where he can imagine.

Men get nervous when the word *submission* is brought up. I can understand the negative connotation it can bring. However, if we are going to *Maximize MENtally* then we can't be so independent that we are above instruction.

Jesus was the greatest example of submission even as he was 100% God and 100% man. He had the ability to perform miracles, heal blinded eyes and change the trajectory of those who were around him; but He knew that His ability to perform and do what He was divinely created to do came only from His Father. Men, we must understand that we are created to be protectors and providers. God has given us all gifts and skills so that we can take care of our families and be a blessing to our homes, communities, churches, even our places of employment. However, we must realize that our ultimate dependence should be on God and not our independence on a temporary earthen vessel. Yes, this is hard for us to accept, but in our independence, we must remember to stay dependent upon God. Proverbs reminds us to, "lean not to our own understanding, but in all our ways acknowledge Him and He will direct our paths." We must remember that even the most skilled person you know needs the grace and covering of God. The man that has more degrees than you still need the grace and the covering of God. The man that seemingly has it all together needs the grace and the covering of God. No man, no matter who it is, is so independent that he doesn't need God's grace and mercy in all that he does.

Our manhood is not merited by how independent we are as men. Manhood is not predicated on what we can obtain. Even more, what we gain is not an indicator of God's hands or presence in our lives, homes or ministries. The basis of our manhood is what we choose to submit to in our independence. We have a daily choice of what and who we will submit to as we pursue this journey of independence. What we submit to shows what has our heart. The next generation of men must see that we need to have hearts submitted to justice and righteousness. For that is the true essence of being an independent man. It makes no sense to be independent without submission. Submission brings about character and a cause.

There was a time in my late 20s when I became arrogantly independent. I was making the money I wanted to make and was able to go where I wanted to go. Because I was finally at the level of independence I had dreamed of, I felt like I could coast and rid myself of God's instructions. Ha! What a joke! I believed that the money I made was an indicator of God's approval of my life; although everything I was doing wasn't in alignment to what I knew was moral and according to the word of God. In my independence, I chose to depend on lying, cheating on my former wife, and other destructive behaviors to cover and keep me. But honestly, it was all carrying me to my grave. I felt like I finally got to a place to where I could literally do what I wanted. No one could tell me anything. In a way, it became narcissistic. I believed that I could do no wrong. Yeah, it was bad. My independence got in the way of my dependence on God. He used people to warn me about my arrogance, but I felt as if it was useless advice. I thought to myself that I was grown,

I'm a man and I could do whatever I pleased. While this was true, it wasn't wise. As a result, God had to strip me of everything to bring my dependence back to Him. It was painful and humbling at the same time.

I did not have a foundation, and as a result I abused the very gift that God had given me. I had nothing to keep me grounded or disciplined in my morals and values. My faith was rocky. I saw my father, in his independence, abuse and destroy everything around him because he did not do the work that it required to heal from the trauma that he faced from his own childhood. That being said, it could've really gone to a dead end concerning me. My dad didn't make it out of his rut. But by the grace of God I did.

Be grateful that God has given you the ability to work and take care of yourself; but remember in your independence you must always stay dependent on Him.

# 5

## _Walking In Freedom_

## _Impact_

Paul urges the believers in Romans 12:2a, "Do not conform to this world, but be ye transformed by the renewing of your mind." As we conclude the journey to *Maximizing MENtally*, we must understand the impact that transforming the mind of a man can have. When the mind of a man is transformed (renewed daily), the man can think clearly, cast vision and lead his family and community. A man with a renewed mind brings progress to his generation and the generations that succeed it.

Now, let's go back to sports for a moment to drive my point home. I'm aware of the mental health crisis that is plaguing the sports industry today. These men who are making millions of dollars are now having to face pressures that many who enjoy the sports they play would never understand. Many of these men come from low-income impoverished homes, and they have seen nothing but crime, chaos and confusion. Many of them depended on their God-given athletic ability to get them out of poverty and into the better lives they live now. Even in that, some men who are playing professional sports are still impacted by what they had to grow up around. We see it far too often, with their horror stories plastered all over the news. Tempers flare over the most minute situations and their anger comes out, more often than not, in front of national audiences. We often don't understand or discern the underlying issues that cause them to want to be swift to throw punches against their defendant or act out in unseemly ways when off the field or court. Furthermore, we often don't understand the impact their acting out has on our boys that are watching these games simply because we enjoy seeing them perform on the field and the court. We don't realize it, but these wounds are being ingrained and perpetuated in our next generation.

However, we as adult men must understand that how we deal with our traumas—publicly and privately—impact those around us; especially the next generation. The impact we make will outlive us and will be remembered by those who encountered us. Fathers of sons, I think it's important to realize that your every move, your every word, and how you handle them directly impacts how your son will treat the next person.

The National Basketball Association understands the impact that mental health has on its league and players. Demar DeRozan—small forward and shooting guard for the San Antonio Spurs—tweeted about his battle with depression. He says, "This depression gets the best of me." Kevin Love talked about his panic attack in 2017 that occurred in the middle of the game against the Atlanta Hawks. He described his panic attack saying, "It was like my body was trying to say to me, 'You're about to die.' I ended up on the floor in the training room, lying on my back, trying to get enough air to breathe." Adam Silver shared his concern about the state of the players' mental health in an interview at the Sloan Conference in Boston according to an article on msnbc.com. It was written by Elijah Shamah and it states, "What strikes me is that a lot of these men are truly unhappy. A lot of these young men are genuinely unhappy." So on September 19, 2019, they put rules in place to ensure the safety of their mental health; including having a full time licensed psychiatrist on the team.

No matter how successful, we must deal with what impacts our behaviors so that we can heal and positively impact those around us. The impact is more valuable than the increase in our salaries and possessions. Trust me, I know this firsthand. How we touch our communities will last longer. Our prayer should be that we impact those around us and that our impact will be one that people can remember and feel good about.

The impact of my dysfunctional upbringing was more than I could take. It affected the decisions I made, the loss of my marriage and the relationships I attracted. The impact of my father not getting healed and not getting the help he needed for himself and his family left a pain that I still find myself grieving over. Healing is a process. However, I realized—after experiencing the challenges that I have faced—that I did not want to leave a negative memory because of my lack of taking care of my mind. The mind is the very tool God has given us to change the trajectory of generations to come. We must guard it and heal it every chance we get. The impact of renewing the mind carries great significance.

I did not understand the impact of my childhood until I got married. A lot of what my father exhibited—that I did not want to repeat—manifested in my behavior when the pressure was on. My consistent adultery, lying and emotional abuse brought pain to my former wife and my daughters who trusted me to be the leader of the home. When I realized the negative impact that this caused, it broke me and caused me to want to turn in a different direction.

To the man who's reading this, it's not too late to heal. It's not too late to start over and leave a positive impact. It's not too late to make it right with your children who saw you make mistakes that impacted them. It's not too late to find resources in your area that will allow you to heal from what it is that impacted you. Men, it's okay to talk about what impacted you. It's there so you can share with your children how to heal from it. Whenever they face challenges that affect their mental health, you can pull on the experience that you've had. It's your testimony. We can no longer hide behind our careers, our cash, clothes, cars or even callings to mask the pain. The results of the unchecked and unhealed wounds of our souls will come out even as we try to hide behind the mask of what it is that we are gifted to do. Gifts and callings do not exempt you from healing. Whether you believe it or not, you have more people rooting for you and that wants to see you positively impact this world because of your healing. Generations are depending on you breaking the façade and healing the wounds. But let me tell you a secret. Above all else, only God can heal you. Learn to depend on

Him and trust His guidance. Yield to the mentors and coaches He sends your way, and let the guard or arrogance and pride down. Then and only then can you truly heal and eventually make an impact on everyone that experiences you and love you.

# *About the Author*

Raymond Forte is a preacher and teacher of the word of God in addition to being a multi-talented singer and musician. Traveling nationally and internationally, Pastor Forte is a highly sought out preacher to boldly proclaim the word and has a great passion for His people. He also is an entrepreneur as he sits the CEO/Founder of Raymond Forte Enterprises, LLC. Pastor Forte currently serves as the "iCitadel" online campus pastor for Citadel of Praise Christian Church in Buckeye and Peoria, AZ under the leadership of Pastor Brian A. Wright.

## _Contact the Author_

Raymond Forte

404-452-4365

raymond.forte1@gmail.com

Facebook, Twitter and Instagram:

@theraymondforte

Made in the USA
Monee, IL
22 April 2023